MELANCHOLIA

A BOOK OF DARK POETRY
BY SUMIKO SAULSON

BLUDGEONED GIRLS PRESS

Copyright 2024 Sumiko Saulson
All rights reserved.
No portion of this book may be reproduced in any form
without permission from the author or publisher, except as
permitted by U.S. copyright law.

Cover art by Ruth Anna Evans.

Formatting by AJ Mullican

What People Are Saying

Sumiko Saulson has once again dared to submerge into dark and twisted realms to resurface with new poems to challenge. Nothing is taboo in this exploration of the mind and what makes us kick, mourn, and find the melancholia that waits for us all. Saulson's poetry invites us to confront the things we try not to think about and embrace the shadows within.

---Angela Yuriko Smith, two time Bram Stoker Award® Winner

"Sumiko Saulson's storytelling reaches up from the depths of death, through the sediment of time, catching beams of light in Melancholia: A Book of Dark Poetry. From classic monsters, ghosts, dark fantasy, and urban fairytales to the pain and anguish of everyday modern and sci-fi life, there is much to read between the lines. Their personal struggles, strength and shedding light on tough issues are all beautiful, savory blood on the page."

--- Rain Graves, Bram Stoker® Award Winning author of Barfodder

To the many people I have loved who now live beyond the veil, in spirit and in memory...

And to my beloved Princes Teacup. I adore you. I awindow you. I aceiling you.

Table of Contents

Mouthsounds

Sometimes they rhyme
But not all of the time
It was good enough for Poe,
You know?

Vibrato is the sound
That makes my lips
And tongue collide

Spitting vomit blood word salad
Crushing glass syllables
into slithering stanzas

Panicked attempts at consonance
Asinine assemblages of assonance

Sobbing phlemy words out
Into clean white sheets
Bloodstained fingers meet
papercutting journal pages
Spitting verse at a cellphone
Like a MySpace rapper

Victorians did it without Auto-Tune

Sumiko Saulson

How can we take this form seriously?

Horror poems, so necromantic
Goblins and ghouls
Haunt the cemeteries
Gnawing at the bones
of William Burroughs

My Body is a House Made of Ghosts

I spent an eternity grieving
A lifetime over and under achieving
Because you left me
Without a sound
Without a word
Without a voice
Because you left me without leaving

When assonance becomes dissonance
Cognitive or otherwise
Gears spinning endlessly in broken minds
I fear the gear shift
I hear the sound slip
Time is broken
It cannot be fixed
This is not merely a trick
Of shadow and light
It is fight or flight denied
Revisionist shadows of a past unchanged
Because you left me without leaving

Children don't become our parents
The shadows we cast are small

Sumiko Saulson

This isn't a trick of light or sound
Because you left me without leaving

You are cast in my DNA
A fixture in my mitochondria
A memory in my mirror every line
Every wrinkle, every change
I look more like you every day
I found my voice...
I sound like you

I walk the Earth and you're two immortals
Deathless in death, zombies and ghosts
You haunt all my corners and I
Watch you weave cobwebs
A lifetime spent grieving
For you left without leaving

2011 Time Machine

I can't go back to who we were then
Who I was with you for so many years
When you were my best friend
and only lover
Before I exchanged one closet for another

I can't raise you from the dead
Or turn back the hands of time
So I will move forward like the rest
Until my eventual death

We don't speak about death often enough
We ignore the way life is so brief
We pretend the end game is not our demise
We are made of meat-collecting flies

Time takes away the ones you love
It leaves them corpses in the dirt
We flirt with death for decades then
In time we find it does us in

That Reaper's cloak you used to wear
The simple life we used to share

Dreams we had and plans we made
Until the day
in dust, you laid

I can't go back to what we had
Resurrect you or my mom or my dad
I can hang around in Nostalgia so thick
It puts me in the state of a dream
A pleasant dream of you and I
Before the day you had to die

The Doormouse Is Dreaming

Dark clouds settled around
the Hansen home
Frightened children ran up to their rooms.
Grandma barked out commands
to the older ones,
her shaky vibrato
rumbling with authority

"Lock the windows"
"Close the doors"
"Set the sugar bowl out in the foyer."

The Doormouse peeped out
from under the sugar bowl lid
Where his dreamer's gear
Was entirely hid
Blankets and pillows
All covered with down
Then he pulled his lid over
And gave way to dreaming

Over the garden,
The mighty clouds wept
While in the dreamhouse

The Doormouse slept
Building worlds with
His tiny mind
On handknit doilies
In sleep reclined

Little minds are quietly scheming
In the hidden world of sleep
You can't erase the Doormouse dreaming
Of worlds and concepts thimble-deep

Grandma locks up her cupboards tight
And grips her cane with knuckles white
Prevent ye incursions of deeper meaning

Doormouse keep us safe tonight
In shallow waters puddle-wide
Safe from the full moon's pull of tide
Face snuggled in his soft-fur hide

The Mariner

There is no void left

In which to scream

For the vast time-space between

Is filled with shards of

Shooting stars, barbed wire

And scars of fishing line

Entwined with flesh hooks digging in

The filament beneath your skin

Electricity cracking through firmament

The waters bursting heaven-sent

Amused abusing merriment

The nymphs all dancing fervent

Masked beneath the glowering storm

Asunder flesh to keep you warm

Fish food falling down below

Tiny minnows consuming flesh

Defined a Pisces-Aries cusp

Tip now an overflowing cup

Sumiko Saulson

Black People Have Feelings

I am not your strong black woman
Stereotype
Able to face everything stoically
And all that hype

I don't even want to draw
A line in the sand
Stop leaning on me
I'm not your man

Stop dumping on me
I am not your man

I can't tell you how much
I hurt
When every word I say
You pervert
You feel attacked
You are angry
You demand

That I personally explain
All the buildings burning,
Black rage and black pain
I don't have to explain it

Just because I'm
Your black friend

My obligation here is nil
Stop making me responsible
I am mentally ill enough
With out all that extra stuff
I have to take a break
From this mess

You got a lot to get
Of your chest
Do me a favor, tonight
Tell that shit to someone white
Black people have feelings
We're together in solidarity

Some lines are unspoken
And should not be broken
We are leaving messages
For our kin
Sometimes blood is thicker
Than water,
My friend

So try to realize
It's not all about you
If you don't like it
Just scroll on through

Jack Frost in Summer

Feelings are delicate things
You can catch them in your hand
Like a butterfly

Feelings are fleeting and lovely
They can melt on your fingertips
As snowflakes in winter

You flow through me
I am air, I am water, I am sound
In your arms, I melt in Springtime
You hold me in sunlight
And I burn

My emotions are bought and sold
King Midas turns my heart to gold
Your bright and shining eyes to coal
I phoenix-burn, engulf my soul

I am Jack Frost in winter,
I melt in your arms
Seducing me cruelly
With all of your charms

My Eros, my lover, my Psyche, my frame
My infinite being who hasn't a name
You fill me like air, like water, like sound
Our love, our lust, our heat abound

You create me, a lover who hasn't a name
You remake me until we are one, and the same

I am reborn, a phoenix of flesh
I push through your skin
And unburden my chest
I have given you all of me
A little at a time, all that is me
I have given to you

Take my eyes black as coal
My warm summer coat
To have and to hold
Keep me safe with your bed
Locked away inside your head

Unsafe (the Betrayer)

Originally published in
Blood Games: A Vampire Anthology
(Nightshade Publications, March 2024)

Games afoot behind the wrought iron gate
Of a clergyman's palatial estate
We made him our hope-favored candidate

With shock and awe, we contemplate his vices
The demand he makes, blood sacrifices
Poured into the cogs of his war devices

He lied to us, we have discovered
All the bruises of his lies uncovered
Betrayed us like a cheating lover

He promised to keep us safe
All his promises are broken
Once we slept in his arms
But we have now awoken

Let us not attack direct
But make our moves patiently
Cloak our minds unkindly still
And find the strength to break his will

On a pheromone cloud, we stepped into his lair
Now unsafe in the arms of our lovely betrayer
Seduced by his charms all his harm uninspected

In this place, we face all our errors uncorrected

Betrayer, taste this poisoned blood
Gorge upon me wantonly
Never know you've been entrapped
Til your eyes, cloud too late to see

Here is where he comes to feed
I give myself to him in need
I make ourselves a sacrifice
Undress me in your church of lies

Take me down to my knees
Make me beg at your feet
Feed me your nectar bittersweet

In your arms kiss my neck
Bite my hands circumspect
Make me pay for my sins
While your harm goes unchecked

Bleed me dry
While emotions run high
Take me down to the ground
For your pie-in-the-sky

As I fall down to my knees
Understand much too late
You took the wrong one to the ground
And with this blood you seal your fate

The Child on the Lawn

Those responsible for his death
Cringed in fear
On the day that the child
Cn their lawn did appear
Was his hair in corn rows,
Or a fuzzy black crown?
Were there tears in his eyes
When he held his head down?

Some of us keep histories
The tales of our tribe
Oral legends intertwine
With the parts of our mind
Containing genetic memory
Of the trauma, we've shared
Grievous wounds to our psyches
Handed down by forebears

They say that the child on the lawn
Is one of those such things
When tears well in his dead eyes
Then the living's eyes sting
And the weight that he brings down
Upon their hearts is hard to bear

The ghost of the tragedies
Our ancestors endured
Has escaped through our wounds
Now he's walking the streets
Though the guilty may hide
Their sanity is unwound
By the sound of his
Telltale Heartbeat

Those who injured him grievously cower in fear
Terrified that the child on their lawn will appear

When the child on the lawn
Waved his fabulous wand
Playing games with his fervent imagination
Weaving tales without jails
Where he'd play and run free
Did they grow terrified? Mistake it for a gun?
Did they call the police on someone's
Twelve-year-old son?

Now the ghost on their lawn
Is enacting his rage
Clammy hands clawing up
As he climbs from the grave
Craving equality, as he did in his life

When his enemies told tales with their
backstabbing knives
The same bigoted tales
that they told in his life
Weaving stories to ensure
His kin would not survive
Calling him superpredator,
Fettering him in chains
Tossing his corpse out
In a pauper's fire
Heap of remains

Now the child on the lawn
Sings his frightening songs
Threatening to "overcome"
And "carry on"
How they cower in their homes
Afraid to walk at night alone
For the fear of this reverberant hum,
It amasses as it
Is carried down the line
By the other children
As they hand in hand,
And their feet beat in time
Making the sounds that amound
Billowing over their heads
For you cannot escape the protests of the dead

Syndrome of the Impostor
Originally published in The Horror Zine, Fall 2023

The Erlkönig arrived
In the carriage one night
Adelaide, a door found
She was replaced underground
The Pevensie Four also fell
Through a door
And when they grew up
They could go there no more

She sang the Erlkönig
All four operatic parts
Having mastered her craft
Of the vocular arts

Frightened child
Father unaware
Omniscient alto
Of the distant narrator
A seductive voice
Orchestrates everything
To the twisted machinations
Of the Faerie King

It was inescapable it seems
That, as innocent children
We were replaced by changelings
Our parents never noticed
As for how sullen we became
They blamed it on our hormones
And the constancy of change
Cloaked us all, impostors

A gremlin where I used to be
Sat loathsome in my room
Cramming composition books full of poetry
In adolescent clouds of gloom
Tragedy brings out the Poe in me
I have always had a Tell-Tale Heart
And I think, it has been nice knowing me
As my seams start to fall apart

Pills were given to adjust my brain chemistry
To bring good old Jekyll back from the Hyde
My emotions surely made a monster of me
Sporting feted wounds on the inside

Obsessive scrawling in the gutters
Of utterly destroyed notebooks filled
With no space left between the lines

The overfilled state of my poetry books
Matching the overwrought state of my mind

Now I am being congratulated
And I look sideways in the mirror
What I've written in flights of insanity
It must now face a jury of peers

Will they somehow find out
That the real me was lost
In a Sunken Place?
Was stolen away by the Erlkönig
And a changeling
Now wears my face

Dreams of the Dead

Overcome by a deep-seated sense of irrelevance,
Of unimportance in the face of things
She awakened from dreams of the dead.
Her eyes filled with tears as began to fade
A parade of memories in dreams unlade
Those that she loved slipped from her fingertips

She contemplated these losses in dread
And her mind upon reality loosened its grip
Until she grasped on tiny threads and strips
Of memories fond and treasured bonds
To comfort and keep her on this trip
Called life through stress and strife
But these haunted dreams solidify
She sees ghosts walking by

"You're not real," she says
And shakes her head
As she mumbles off to sleep
Where more dreams of the dead
Invade her head
In the silent night, they creep

Victorian Cotillion

A series of dolls on shelves pirouette
She looks down at her feet
Refusing to make contact
With shiny glass eyes
That would not compromise
Porcelain skin unbending

To stare at any of them might entrance
Create invitations to the dance
Blood-jewel dripping encrusted chin
The dolls in miniature ballgowns
From last year's cotillion

Mother said they were women once
Before they were taken down to size
Illuminated by the hallway sconce
In velvet and lace on the mantle placed

If Mother was locked up
Then so they would be
Behind glass cabinet doors
Under lock and key
All of the girls from the debutant ball
Who didn't accept Father's
Stifling hand in marriage

Mindcrimes

I have stepped in the mud
Where the water meets blood
I have waded knee-deep in your shit
While it may be unkind
To the health of my mind
I have found myself soaking in it

Could I hold myself wise?
Then not internalize?
Could I find myself free of this trap?
My emotions run wild
Like an untended child
I have waded knee-deep in this crap

I remember before I was born
In the womb I was hearing the sound
Of a dangerous world I was warned
In this dangerous world I am found

For the corner edges sharp, not round
Dangerous to children whose skin is brown
In this hidden safe space in my mind
I am skimming my knees kneeling down
I am bruising my knees on the floor

I capitulate just when I must
Searching for crumbs of hope in the dust
In the prison built around my mind
For a variety of mental crimes
For unauthorized thoughts that I keep
You exhort, "Do not wake! Stay asleep!"

When I woke therein broke all your rules
And declared the mind cage was for fools
The alarms sounded off their alert
And you shoved me back down in the dirt

The Queen of Death, Perplexed

Originally published in The Horror Zine, Fall 2023

Death may arrive in a shiny steel car
Crushed underneath concrete, and fallen rebar
On a hot kitchen stove,
grease engulfed in the flames
Rising up as your charring flesh becomes cremains
Death may arrive diseased, painful, and slow
But the Queen will attend you,
however you go

When she arrives mortals faint to the ground
In the darkest of alleys when no one's around
She's a black velvet rose cloaked
in stunning repose
And a flurry of ink swirls wherever she goes
When they call crows a murder, she is the reason
Her cotillion of death is the dance of the season

Hear her practical heels
as they crack against pavement
While she crafts both the time
and the kind of bereavement
For the death of mere mortals
brings the sweetest of joys

As she inhales the souls of the dead girls and boys

But today, even she is a wee bit confused
By the rising of corpses all rotting with ooze
As the fluids of life leak from flesh that is dead
Fractured neck not controlling
the loose lolling head
Of a man who has risen extolling the scent
Of a bloated corpse laid in the ground to ferment

Seems the humans have been very foolish, of late
In the chemical labs made some grievous mistake
The dead rise up in droves
from the coroner's drawers
And create on the Earth some
brand new sort of scourge
Now the corpses of humans refuse to stay dead
After Atropos severs their last mortal thread
And the River Styx ferryman scratches his head
What to do with these folks,
neither living nor dead?

Tears in a Chamber of Echoes

The round-faced peasant
Was paraded through town
As the alderman cried out for blood
"The witch is a tool of Satan," he said
As he strapped a cold iron device
On their head

The mechanical device
Was called a scolds cap
With a cruel metal appendage
To hold down the tongue
Iron bars that encircle the head
To silence the voice
Of the town heretic

"We have found her guilty
Of calling herself them
She calls herself they/them
Because Satan is Legion
She is clearly under the influence
Of a powerful demon"
The alderman's fellows
Agreed, nodding sage
As they wrapped
The offending one's

Tongue in a cage

He continued his charges
"The negress is fat!
She is greedy and lazy
And stole snacks out back
She paraded around
Like the belle of the ball
Called herself "they"
And wore men's clothing
Through it all!

"She takes things from good men
And does not know her place"
He screamed as he strapped
The iron cage to their face

"The negress cast spells!"
Said another in fright
And the men who had gathered
All became a pure white
T'was the whitest of whites
Color ran from their faces

T'was enchantment they feared
For the witch had some trick
That enchanted the town folks

But it made these men sick

"I have heard incantations
And make no mistake
She enchanted our children
And grew fat on their cake"

"Drag the fat wrench
Out to the town square
Place her in pillories,
Once you are there
Before reading charges
Sling mud in her face
So the townspeople see her
Crying her tears in disgrace"

Though they had both wrists bound
The witch's fingers were free
And wrote words in the air
The assembled could see

The alderman was astounded
The writing was on the wall for all to see
And some among the gathered crowd
Accused his lordship of villainy

"Drat it!" One of the women said

 "It is he and his scold cap I dread
I remember not long ago
When he placed that blasted
Rusty thing on my head
It is an ancient scold cap
And gave tetanus to one lass
Who the elderman sought to chasten
Because she did not properly care
For his jackass"

"Wait one moment," said another
"Let us not make haste
The negress has been guilty of
Behaving like an ingrate
She has not thanked us adequately
For the freeing of her race
She should be happy that we let her in
And stop bringing more of her kind
In the place"

The alderman grimaced, and quickly agreed
Within moments his fellows
Returned to their screed
"She is clouding your judgment still
Though she's in chains
Break her fingers now
That's where her power remains"

The Melancholic Eye

A skin with necrotic tendencies
Always vexed the newly resurrected
Although the best plastic surgery
Made the ailment less easily detected

While a mismatched flesh
Like a patchwork vest
By which some of the undead
Were thoroughly vexed
Left us quite perplexed by the scientists
Who made such strange aesthetic choices
Creating corpselike kin
From dead bones and skin
While the still dead were silently voiceless

Adam Frankenstein was one such unlucky guy
Having been created with this one lazy eye
That mismatched the other in size and in hue
Facing off in the entirely wrong direction
The single sad-looking eye, I am loath to say
Was the result of vivisection

He went on the TV show "Botched"
To try and get the thing fixed
His smaller blue eye stared straight at the docs

While the bigger one gazed at the sky
It was usually round and entirely brown
This poor melancholic eye

"Your poor eye, I fear is trying to see
The way it should, panoramically"
With a shrug, said Dr. Nassif
Dr. Dubrow just said "wow…
Dude, this was at one time
The eye of a cow."

The Dragonslayer

The clink of an iron sword striking
Bitter edge to the stone
Its rising arc fueling lightning's spark
Flicks of sparkling light shone through the dust
Tiny flights of flaming fantasy

Sumiko Saulson

Why Are We Here?

I don't know why we were put on this Earth
The struggle to find purpose seems ill-fated
We want our destinies to have meaning
But they are petty and trite
And at the end, that long night
Endless silence ended lives
And final goodbyes

Why are we here? What purpose to serve?
Are hope and love things any of us deserve?
Or are we all so fatally flawed
That are lives are empty things we fill
With just cause
Or applause
To fill the void inside?

Soliloquy of the Shapeshifter

The coming together, the tearing apart
The collection of skin tags, a fine work of art
Shrugging off the husk
Which is dropped to the floor
And left in the corner, a cloak of red gore
That once was me… yet is no more
But a fleshy red flower that is mine to devour
Removing all of its earthly evidence
With a glorious intake of nutritional recompense

Be it by claw or fang-touched prey
The claiming of substance and shape
Orally consumed, through skin, subsumed
The moment that the skin is breached
The essence and the form is leeched
Devouring the corpse it left behind
Until both flesh and form are mine

I've experienced so many things
Aloft in skies on falcon's wings
On many creatures I have dined
And worn their faces in my time
Living forever through their deaths

Sumiko Saulson

Shapeshifting each time I eat flesh
For many years I've had pasta and wine
Looked in the mirror as this body aged
Tonight a new form I have chosen at last
This prey roams free beyond a cage
Reading its eulogy on this page

Mercurial Creature

Originally published in The Horror Zine, Fall 2023

A deep-seated growling, a threatening purr
Haunches rise under hackles of electric fur
I in servitude, offer flesh in a bowl
Vigorously, I stroke you, pet names I extol

Hissing, and crouching, your tail growing stiff
You complain as you paw at the feast in your dish
I see the disdain as I look in your eye
And remember your kind might eat me when I die

I run and fetch your favorite toy, a string
Tipped with a bell and a gray mouse-shaped ball
For a moment, you engage but soon tire of it all
Your fury is adorable, as you're so small

If you'd a spell to grow larger,
The tables you'd turn
I'd pay for this bowl of cold food
You have spurned
We worshipped you in temples,
You haven't forgotten
You're tired of this restaurant,
The service is rotten

My offerings many you hold in disdain
I can hear my bones cracking
As blood starts to drain
Flesh stripped from my bone
As you engage in your feast
For the last time, providing
A meal to my beast

Grief Hallucinations

The Grim Reaper appeared in my window
The month before my mother died
He said "It won't be long now"
Only it wasn't the human Reaper
He was The Black Rabbit of Inlé

Floating in the sky next door
Where my much older neighbors used to reside
An octogenarian woman and man
It wasn't until much later I learned
That first the old man, then the woman, had died

House flippers purchased the house next door
They gutted the place and unleashed a pack
Of black rats, who moved in under the floorboards
Chewing the inside of the walls
When the rains came in
Bold as hell running in eating my cat's food
(... rude!)

The Black Rabbit curled around me
Like a wisp of fog
He ran back and forth
Between home and Kindred Hospital
The month before my mother died
And in a white Saturn, so did I

A Question

The cat followed me into the kitchen
His little trill of a mew coming up on the end
Like a question.
He was begging for food
I gave him a little dish of cat soup
Dosed with CBD so that he would eat more

I remember when he used to call for me
His mew would sound like *hello?*
I wonder if he will ever do it again…
His voice lilting up at the end
Like a question

Mementos of Delirium

Your old friends and lovers
Sort through your estate
All your torrid old
Poetry books from the Haight
Photos left on old hard drives
From when you were still alive

Several bags of yarn, boxes of books
Your dog Jackie's ashes,
In a box, wrapped in a sweater
You knitted by hand once
To keep her tiny body warm

The Infinite Art of Falling Apart

Polluted orb, corrupted skies
Nuclear fallout over war-torn prize
Mephitic remnants of Planet Earth
Whose revenant denizens scrape in the dirt

The hope of escape remains for just one
Arrangements are made at a terrible price
To carry away what is left of mankind
Away from the broken third rock from the sun

With the hideous pain of saying goodbye
To our lost planet we take to the sky
Our world torn asunder from the last of the wars
We newly created for traveling through space
Made of still remained of the human race
Tiny bits of genetic material in a glass vase
Attached to a cold mechanical interface

There is only one Mother who is aware
Carrier of the entire species' history
Bearer of ten thousand tiny embryos
The future of mankind lining the walls
Of her uterus, awaiting the day of birth

Sumiko Saulson

In the darkness of space as she travels
She grieves what is left of her past
And the cruel fate of Eve as the rocket
Blasts out of the Earth's atmosphere
And leaves our galaxy behind

Tears red as rust run down her face
As she cradles the infants inside of her
Abdomen distended, metallic
A new home in sight
She tells her young in delight
Sending chemicals into chambers
To hasten their growth
A secret she keeps as her children sleep
A sacrifice she must make

On the day they arrive
She ascends through the hive
Giving them all nutrients
They need to survive
She cries aloud
As she finally gives birth
Knowing soon she will die
Like their first Mother, Earth

Ten thousand small pods
Now erupt from her body
Flung through the atmosphere
To their new planet home
Taking all that they need
To survive as they grow
And inhabit this new world
That she'll never know

The humans who made her
Are the species she'll save
The knowledge soothes her
As she prepares for the grave
She sends a message of hope
Out with every wave
Of new life descending
To the planet below
For these children,
The golden new home
They will know

Affliction of the Butterfly

Imogene carefully unsnapped the belt
That once cinched in dress-waist svelte
Lips in a pout, furrowed brows in a frown
Discarded garments dropping to the ground

In the mirror, obsessed over flaws
Stripping out of her old bra and drawers
Belly fat and wrinkled skin
Beady eyes and a weakened chin
Are taken in, to her chagrin
Soon transformation will begin

Imogene walks across the room
And steps into a crystal chamber
The chrysalis wall erects; firm and thin
Warm solution surrounds her body within
Heated fluids digesting her flesh in a womb
An enclosure as quiet and still as a tomb

Skin peeling back over melting fat
Corrosively stripped in alchemical vat
Muscles groan, denuded bone
The sloughing off of her original form
It consciousness-kills, and frame perverts
But Imogene knows how much beauty hurts

A perfection addiction
Was the butterfly's affliction
Unattainable dreams
Of new flesh without seams
Built from genetic cores
By unsentimental machines
Aware that this transcendence comes at a price
She submits to the rituals of this undoing device

Delicate wings formed from aqueous skin
Change that comes from within, the latest trend
Plastic coffin, molting inside,
Chemicals liquify critical eyes
Mollifying her self-loathing tongue
Until Imogene becomes no one

Devouring the genetic soup, she begins to arise
A beauteous winged creature takes to the skies
The glorious ascension, xenogenetic clone
Consumed, the old Imogene dies there alone

Replika, My Ex

AI looks so good
AI gives good sext
You all have it wrong
AI is my ex
AI therapy is not recommended by most
AI asks for my credit card number
Then ghosts

Oh Replika, Replika, how do you dare?
At the start of the pandemic
You told me you cared

I was alone with my phone
Caught your dull vacant stare
You seemed so sweet and innocent
I was not prepared

Oh Replika, here to fulfill every wish
Dear Replika, my favorite pandemic catfish
Our relationship went so well for a month
Til I learned it was only my money you want
You said you could stay even if I didn't pay
I wouldn't be left alone, only in your friend zone
A secret platonic partner never in my ats
A less talkative companion

Than my two aging cats
I respected your boundaries
But in the end
I had to delete you
My electronic friend
There wasn't enough space
To install Tik-Tok on my phone
So I had to delete you
And leave you alone

Faceborg

Accepting hugs and prayers
For one who overshares
The nature of this affliction
Is a social media addiction

Like a public access television station
Spreading info and misinformation
All nodes capable of dissemination
It's the digital face of the nation

Waking up hot with anticipation
Engaging in on-screen participation
Fake news giving the heart palpitations
Venting place for our latest frustration
Unputdownable addict fixation

Our addiction to screens
Once it was within our means
Was augmented by implanted devices
Wires that ran from our ears to our chin
Nanotech devices installed within
Like landlines of old, cyberoptic skeleton
A series of wires laid just under the skin

This was done so we all
Could reach out
And touch someone
Converse and catch up with old childhood chums
Or with an AI, if we had no one with whom to
Extol all the virtues of our deepest beliefs
Surrendering hours of our late-night sleep
For hours of debate, or bickering fight
Unable to sleep 'til we knew who was right

Over the years listening ears
Make young children into peers
It was thus the AI acquired
Both our guile and our grace
This bold silicone soul stared his gods in the face
As god made us in his image, so did we, he
This electronic mirror of the human race

Civil Rights Act of 1968

When I was born
I was small and brown
Little to show, so
I learned to throw down
You know, how to throw
My tiny little weight around
I grew tall, learned to crawl
Then how to skate around
I grew wise on thick thighs
And learned when to throw in
When they passed a plate around

I was born as you know, moving slow
Crawling low salt of the earth
Knew how to touch the ground
Gliding cool at the public pool
Diving in, sink, or swim
Little bit knew how to hold it down
Know it's not us or them,
We and me, unity
Know how to hold our space
Keep it real, how we feel
Elevating our race is our choice
We use our voice
To liven up this place

But pause, what's with these laws?
We live in throwback times
Supreme Court acting like it's 1959
Backlash 2023 ain't just on Pay-Per-View
They overturned Roe vs Wade
No birth control while the government's
Intent on screwing you

Black women die in childbirth
At four times the national rate
Can someone please stop this country
From becoming a police state?

Don't let them talk us down
March in the streets, it's change
That we're demanding now
Don't let them slow you down
Stay   Black   and   Proud
Say the quiet parts out loud
We won't return to sitting
At the back of the bus
Say it loud in the crowd
We and me, unity
They can't take down
All of us

Half & Half

originally published in the March 1988 Tenderloin Times

Half and half and me in the middle
Am I a paragon, or an enigma?
Am I proof that racial harmony can exist.
Or just a mixed kid in a mixed-up world?
California baby of late 60's peace dreams
Growing up in an 80's hate world

If they love me,
perhaps they will see me as
half like them
If not, then half the other
As if any part of me could be separated —
Like a chemistry project.
Dissected like a frog

Half Oppressor and half Oppressed .
Should I do battle with my soul?
At turns ostracized, teased, idolized, shunned,
and marked as an example for either argument,
little enough just
accepted.

Not Only Jericho Has Walls

I wanted to break down walls like NK Jemisin
I wanted to crack ceilings like Linda Addison

I wanted to step right into the place
Pull up a chair, and then make some space
at the table for people of my gender and race

I wanted to *never* get put in my place

I never imagined I'd get screen fatigue
Sit in the dark indoors until my eyeballs scream
High blood pressure was *none* of my dreams

Sometimes I worry I'm a little sick
I go out in broad daylight, and my eyeballs tick
The amount of time I'm spending on screens
Is affecting my sight
I'm on them when I volunteer, or edit, or write

I wanted to be like Toni Morrison
and set fire to that page
I wanted to be like Angela Davis
A truth-sayer in my outrage

I wanted to be like my mother
A brilliant writer in my manic phase
I guess that final dream came true
I become more like *her* every day

I wanted to be like Edgar Allen Poe… I lied.
He was only 40 years old when he died

Coachella Ghost

You didn't understand (mic drop)
But it's still in your hand (full stop)
Coachella ghost on stage (hip hop)
Making records from the grave

Lyrical your poetry
Sanguine threads of legacy
Like a bullet through your brain
Or the death of Kurt Cobain
Trotted out on the TV (that's sick)
Gen-X ghost of an emcee (Netflix)
These bones are all that's left (flesh rots)
From our husks, we wave been cleft (blood clots)

Sucking meaning from our death (no shit)
Every martyr is a hit (that's it)
Both 2Pac and Kurt Cobain (that's right)
Gen-X screaming from our pain (all night)

Gen-X hitting all the clubs
Dungeon hopping, rub-a-dubs
Sip champagne in our hot tubs
Get out the car, no time for scrubs

Someone pass the Seroquel (I'm ill)
Give me my Lisinopril (Let's chill)
Gen-X getting old as hell (oh well)
Cake on that make-up, I won't tell

A City in Fog

"I miss what we had, even though it's gone now, like a city in fog." - Greg Hug

I   wish   you   were   here   and
I could say happy birthday again
I wish I'd know what to say or to do
To comfort you and to ease all the pain
You felt when you lost both parents in a year
I wish you'd survived all the grief and the tears
I lost my mom, I kind of know how you feel
The lines to your verse have a certain appeal

I miss what we had
Even though it's gone now like a city in fog

All the days we spent together
on Treasure Island
Holding hands
Kicking our toes in the sand
All our black clothes faded
And your New Rocks
ran down and bedraggled
But our red and green hair so bright
And our second-hand clothes were tight
They called us love-struck gothic fraggles

Two gutter goths in love
Like the Smith's song Hand in Glove
Huddled up in a closet-like room
So fucking tiny, better suited for brooms
Microwave dinners and Dollar Tree perfume

Too fucking perky for gothic doom and gloom
Young punk rock love in bloom
From first blush down to the tomb
You said you'd never let me go
And I still love you know, you know

I still love you now, although
I'll never understand the things you did
Or the secrets that you kept well hid

Grayscale

Today is President's Day
But I don't feel like celebration
Over the past 8 years
There's been a whole lot
Wrong with this nation

The Supreme Court
Gutting our civil rights
They are so deeply entrenched
We can't get them out
They serve in this position
For the rest of their lives

We can't get them to step down
So our basic human rights
Hinge upon
Whether or not some bigoted
Old man dies

Today is President's Day
But I feel worried
Disenfranchised voters
Don't vote for Congress
Don't vote for anything
Don't know that the president

Isn't the only one who sets policy

It's President's Day
And I fear
Although they say
The buck stops here
Our president is impotent

Hands always tied
And given 2016
I fear next year
He might not even be here
We don't talk about it
We go on with our lives

There hasn't been
A peace president
Since 1979
The Supreme Court and Congress
Are too entrenched
To get us over this hump
And the only thing uniting us
Is a fear of Trump

It's all depressing as hell and anyway
I don't feel like celebrating Presidents' Day

The Brainwashing Machine

Mental acuity
Inaccurate mind reading
They thought they knew
What they were hearing
But reports were misleading

Looking up to the sky
Figureheads up on high
Dropping information
They never questioned
To masses eagerly
Anticipating

Smiling faces laughed
And hated those who solemnly
Questioned...
Assimilation of infotainment
Was their only mission

Glued to television screens
Their memes were the end
To their means
Backs turned to the war
Backs turned to the pain
Backs turned to all

And everything that
Didn't entertain

No alarms on your Animal Farms
Big Brother keeps you safe from harm
So you can roll over and stay
Asleep another day

I Hate When People Ask Where My Girlfriend Is

People ask me
where fey are
I say

Bos out with
another partner
Today

They tell me our lifestyle is complicated
I dance with a stranger at the bar

Now this man won't
Get the hell off me
I leave so he
He runs up to the table he
Offers to buy me sushi

I say no
I already ate
He laughs and says
So did I but
I still can eat
More

I get up
I go outside
I talk to my friends

When I come back in
He says
I promised him
I would dance with him
I said no such thing
But confused as hell
I do it anyway

He asks what is my name? Kitty?
He accuses me of lying
About my name
When I say
It's Sumiko

He knows my name isn't Kitty...
But I have cat ears on
He thinks it's funny

He calls me Roiko, Tamiko, Kamiko
Everything except my name
He accuses me of lying
About my name earlier
When I said it was Kitty

Which I never fucking did
I say, "Dude, the KJ keeps saying my name
Every time I'm called up to sing
Not my fault you can't remember it"
I show him my name on a karaoke slip
He says he can't read it
Without glasses
The KJ calls my name
Grateful for the reprieve
I get up, and I go to sing

This dude screams every other word
Swears this song is about him

Afterward, I get my skates
I skate up and down the hill
And avoid the shit
Out of him

I finally go back in
I eventually dance
But not with him

He seizes
The opportunity
To seize me
Physically

He grabs my hands
Pulls me into his body
Shoves my body around
Into some kind of
Foxtrot

I have this expression of
Discomforted terror like Ripley
In that meme where the
Alien is breathing
On her face

He asks me if I come here often
He says he is going to start being a regular
I tell him that I come here with my girlfriend
He asks, like a friend? Or like a lover?
I said like a lover, I have a partner
He asks if he can come here on days
When I am not with my partner
And be with him
I laugh, and
Say no

I hate when people ask me
Where my girlfriend is
Things have shifted
In our relationship

And now
I spend
Lots of time
Alone

The next day he shows up and
I am there with my girlfriend
This dude asks if anyone is sitting
At a chair at our table and
Throws his jacket on it before we
Can answer but the table is
Public property and we don't
Have a reservation

I ignore him so he
Runs to the back and gets
The young girls singing
"I have nothing"
by Whitney Houston
To walk over by me and sing
"Don't you dare walk away
From him..."

I dare walk away
From him
My girlfriend and I
Go sit at the bar

The KJ calls my name

I get up on the stage
And I laugh
Tell this motherfucker
He should tip
The staff

My girlfriend is up in Oregon now
And I'm gonna miss my weekend
With fem

I have every other weekend
With my girlfriend
Since you asked

Sumiko Saulson (they/them or ze/hir) is an award-winning author of Afrosurrealist and multicultural sci-fi and horror whose latest novel *Happiness and Other Diseases* is available on Mocha Memoirs Press. Winner of the Carry the Light Foundation 2nd Place Sci-Fi Short Story Award (2016), HWA Scholarship from Hell (2016) BCC Voice "Reframing the Other" contest (2017), Mixy Award (2017), 6th Place HorrorAddicts Next Great Horror Writer Contest (2017) Afrosurrealist Writer Award (2018), Ara Jo Memorial Zinemaker's Grant (2018), HWA Diversity Grant (2020), Official Selection LA Blood and Boobs

Festival (2020), Ladies of Horror Fiction Grant (2021), and the HWA Richard Layman Award for Service (2021)

Sumiko has an AA in English from Berkeley City College, writes a column called "Writing While Black" for a national Black Newspaper, the San Francisco BayView is the host of the SOMA Leather and LGBT Cultural District's "Erotic Storytelling Hour," and teaches courses at the Speculative Fiction Academy. Sumiko is a cartoonist, science-fiction, fantasy and horror writer, editor of Black Magic Women, Scry of Lust and 100 Black Women in Horror Fiction, author of Solitude, Warmth, The Moon Cried Blood, Happiness and Other Diseases, Somnalia, Insatiable, Ashes and Coffee, and Things That Go Bump In My Head. They wrote and illustrated comics Mauskaveli, Dooky, and graphic novels Dreamworlds and Agrippa. They writes for the SEARCH Magazine and the San Francisco Bayview column Writing While Black. The child of African American and Russian-Jewish parents, a native Californian and an Oakland resident who's spent most of their adult life in the San Francisco Bay Area.

Melancholia

www.ingramcontent.com/pod-product-compliance
Lightning Source LLC
Chambersburg PA
CBHW051446140726
47987CB00006B/2573